To Whom Much Is Given Much Is Expected

The Greatest Assets Are Perhaps The Catalyst-Gifts

Loran Joly

ReEnvision Press

Contents

Chapter One

To Whom Much Is Given Much Is Expected - A Christian text to ponder

> *"To Whom MUCH is GIVEN, Much is Expected"*

Luke 12:48

These words are from the Christian Scriptures.

***

They were also the driving force which led Dr. Albert Schweitzer to go to Africa as a medical missionary and more.

***

Now, one might ponder, the next time we see someone with apparently great gifts, and who doesn't seem to be utilizing them for the benefit of others that much, this question:

Just what gifts are we talking about?

Are these gifts of money?

Gifts of a "great schooling"?

Gifts of being well loved, or as Dr. Winnicott put it, loved well-enough?

Or the gift of a stable childhood?

***

Indeed, as per this article,

"What does it mean that "to whom much is given, much will be required" (Luke 12:48)?"

https://www.gotquestions.org/much-given-req uired.html

Chapter Two

Is it "In the Genes?

And what, in general, creates the so-called Geniuses throughout history?

And this including the great Religious Geniuses, one might say?

To include those who do great artistic work, writing work, political work, music work, dance work, and philosophical work, or comedy work, say?

What, say, enables a few to create that Great American Novel, as they call it?

Or to go to Hollywood and become a profound star, whom we then call someone with Star Quality or a Box Office Draw, or who is termed highly Charismatic, in the good sense?

***

Some say it's simply "Inheritance", of a Genetic nature: "It was in their genes"....

Others say these persons "Met the right people" along the way, in life.

Others attribute it, in shorthand, to this phrase: "They were born with a Silver Spoon in their Mouths."

Or, "Their brain has "Unusual Wiring", or "weighs more than other brains do"....

Or, "We will never know"....

Chapter Three

Some Great Persons to Consider?

I would have to say, though, that I have observed some key traits in great persons throughout history, and mention certain Traits or Gifts – or Catalysts – that they likely had - in the following chapter.....

I am including persons such as:

- Einstein.

- Dostoyevsky.

- Political "Greats": I will leave names out for now....

- Various Religious sages and more....

- Ralph Waldo Emerson and Henry David Thoreau.

- Dr. Albert Schweitzer.

Chapter Four

Gifts and the MEGA-GIFTS of CATALYSTS

So, after pondering, pondering, and yet more pondering, I have come up with these ideas on what "Separates the Absolute Greats from the Rest of Earth's Greats....

I refer to what I call MEGA-Gifts.

And in turn, another term I create,

The CATALYST-Gifts.

***

Why do I use the term "Catalyst"?

Because in Chemistry, there is the idea that without a Catalyst, nothing much happens.

Things stay rather the same.

Things stay Inert, one might say.

***

But apply a CATALYST, and WHAM,

It's like a MULTIPLIER had been applied, to not just 10x things, but 1,000x things.

So, again, I call these, "CATALYSTS":

***

I list these below, and while this is so seemingly simple, in number of words used, I think the following bears due consideration:

And as time permits, I can develop these much more: but for reasons of family and health, I simply mention them in the briefest fashion.

THESE ARE the MEAT of this BOOK, in fact.

- Massive Time-on-Hand: (Einstein worked seemingly 24/7 on his theory of Relativity for 20 years, and needed to teach only a couple of lectures a week for his daily monetary needs.) Often from a combination of a handicap which repels most people, and some steady funding from some source, indefinitely. This also promotes massive time for Observing.

- Abject financial poverty, which forces a person to build Internal Power to combat one's fears, rather than $-Power or Ally-Power or Manipulative Power.

- Massive Mathematical talents: but only inasmuch as applied to understanding *People*, not for building monetary wealth, or furthering fame, or even the solving of some medical calamity.

- Massive verbal skills - so massive that these can be developed only by having high mathematical skills to create the vocabulary out of thin air..

- MASSIVE SUFFERING - of a sort that no one would sign up for, as "Training" - thus going beyond even "Navy Seal Training" - which is almost NECESSARY, for one to Question All that we are taught us by Parents and Marketings, as the Supposed-Best-Way to Be Happiest.... It is thus Matrix-Ripping Pain which - and only which - can cause us to Examine Everything we were both Taught in the Past, and are being Exposed to, in the Present, as The Best of the Best in our world today.

- Finally, a whole lot of Isolation from Toxic Ideas, Toxic Vocabulary, and Toxic People-Influences.

To my parents, who made this possible.

For instance, my mother, an immigrant from eastern Poland, having come to America at the age of
twelve, after a two week long boat journey, to Ellis
Island....

*My mother as a young gal in Europe,
before coming to America*

And to my father, too, a most astute Trainer in

life....

Brought up in the ghettos of Philadelphia; left school at the age of seventeen; and later acquired a GED and went on to obtain a Ph.D. degree at a major University in English Literature; who thus led to my interest and pursuit of writing at a very early age; and too, with respect to his love of photography, both of these areas, too, rubbing off on me: hence, "The apple doesn't fall far from the tree"?

Training!

Then, too, my grandparents:
For significantly, my grandmother raised me during my first four years, in my waking hours. And

her husband – my grandfather – worked in the tool and die industry for cars; she, born in eastern Poland, like my mother, and was a farmer there; he, born in Odessa, Ukraine, and a Mennonite, and herb-collector and maker of many grandfather clocks in his spare time, on their farm in Michigan:

*Grandparents in Niagara
Falls, I believe*

And to my farm experience, as a youth, each summer, in Michigan:

*My great-grandmother, and my
mother, and I, when I was seven or so,
on my grandparent's farm*

Then, too, to a man of most great impact upon

myself, too, from the ages of twelve to fourteen,

starting when I first sought him out to help me

obtain a ham radio license at that age of twelve:

Mr. Foster; who interestingly did have a foster child he raised when I knew him; he helped me obtain my ham license; he hunted; he took me to ham conventions and camped with me; he collected stamps and coins; and let me build electronic projects in his workshop; and even took me for a ride on his motorcycle, popping a wheelie

And finally, to "Religion":

Again, that of my grandmother, a Baptist; and my grandfather, a Mennonite from Ukraine - born in the city of Odessa.

The ethnic Baptist church I at-
tended in the summers, when
a youth, while on the farm the
other six days of the week... Ger-
man was spoken....

And to my parents' religious influence upon myself, too: for they almost became missionaries in the
Plymouth Brethren Church – a group similar to
the Amish, Mennonites, and Quakers: they were
to be posted to Canada.

And to L'abri, started by Francis Schaeffer.
Whereupon I spent a week in training at the Mass-
achussettes branch, in 1982.

And later, other faiths, too....

Including the faith of the Native Amerian Indians, whom I first came into contact with when living in California, having spent time exploring Arizona, and too, in Cherokee, North Carolina and Vonure, Tennessee:

A photograph I made while visiting the Cherokee Indian Reservation in 2021, camping nearby for four days in a tent, in the Blue Ridge Mountains

I made a visit to Vonure, Tennessee, in 2021, to learn more about the Cherokee Indians. Amongst the sights was the Sequoya Birthplace Museum, featuring Sequoya, who had single-handedly created the Cherokee alphabet, under great duress. I again camped, this time in the Cherokee National Park near Vonure, for several days

Possible Typos! A Small Mini-Book on Perfectionism Perhaps?

This is what one might call a White Paper, or Musing, too, or Rough Draft, ...

And thus, is not Polished; or Utterly-Complete; and too, of course, both a Hypothesis and is Subject to Revision and Change of Mind.

YET, PUT OUT in UN-Polished FORM, DUE to ...

The probability of a car accident, or stroke, or heart attack, or cancer, or Alzheimers' striking the author.

As well as the importance of this topic, and in view of all the other writings that this author already has "piled up", ready to press the print button on, almost literally.

And to high level of "content" – generating, overall.

***

Or, to put it another way,

This book has blemishes!

Call them typos, or meanderings, or other Fingerprints.

Or lack of Airbrushing. Varnishing.

***

Why?

Perhaps best put, is because I don't have the time, energy, and youthhood, for it to be the Ut-most-Best.

Or as some have said, hence, "80% = Done".
Or, "Good – Enough".

Or, "A bird in the hand is worth two in the bush".
Put another way, Better with blemishes, than nothing at all...
Or, too, better, a slightly blemished Apple a Day, than NONE, for MONTHS and even YEARS.

***

Noting, too the commonplace Typos in everyday areas we pursue, each as to what most Floats our Boats:

For some, football games, as an example: for at a football game, there are the blemishes – the typos – of cold weather, hot weather, loudness from some-one stocked to of Mead, and possible rain or snow …. I know this from having attended a very frigid Minnesota Vikings football game when a child, growing up in Minnesota, and when playing golf, too, as a teen, in November, with hands chapped from the cold to the point my knuckles bled – yet I played on, despite the knuckle-typos, so to speak.

Similarly, some might find a partner to have some challenging traits to cope with – call these Typos, if you will – but stay in the partnership for the overall best payoffs.

And same for jobs / careers – that boss we find so challenging, or certain co-workers, or certain customers, or the physical setting of the workplace overall, could well be termed Typos.

***

Even our children can be said to have "Typos"; and our Parents, too; and in-laws.

Or our favorite politician or talk show host or minister or spiritual leader, or philosopher, or psych-writer or novelist....

Yet we carry on: we, if Mature, decide and commit to not Throwing Out the Baby With the Bathwater – or put another way,

THROWING OUT the BABY with the TYPOS.

***

We don't THROW OUT the GOOSE that LAYS GOOD-ENOUGH EGGS, hence?

Because we have come to realize that we cannot likely EVER find – on PLANET EARTH, anyway – a PERFECT CAKE that we can EAT, TOO.

***

Perhaps for those who are familiar with certain terms, might this be called "SPLITTING"?

The Author

The author resides in Kentucky,

The author does not have a Ph.D. or an MD degree. Nor is he a college graduate – for he does not consider his four years at West Point to be a college, and his four years at Berea College, studying solely athematics, were as a community member at the half time level, and no degree was ever thus awarded....

***

These are some of his credentials....

The author's influences include ...

Key aspects of the author's life have included...

Last day at West Point
in 1983

*Berea College grounds, where I was
the Ponderer of the Math department,
studying only mathematics at the ages of
forty-one through forty-five, and tutor-
ing for the Berea College Mathematics
Department, to pay off all my tuition
at this scholarship-only college. Here I
first learned to use a computer; and purchased my first cellphone: both at the
young age of forty-one...*

It was here that I continued my photography work, and including joining the local photo club, where I met a Mr. Warren Brunner, the town's portrait photographer, who I reconnected with in 2021 and was greatly encouraged by; he was instrumental in my future photo efforts, and a year after meeting with him frequently in 2021 and during 2022, I first started keeping a portfolio of images on Fine Art America's website; and then, started creating photo books on places in Kentucky; and then started a Shopify store in late 2022, too, to sell these.

One of many buildings at Berea College

Photograph of my mother, left, at the age of two; my grandmother, center, and a helper, right, 1940, as war refugees in Poland, during World War II

And, my summers at my European relatives'
farm in Michigan, during my childhood years...

*Author's great-grandmother, in
background; mother, right, and
myself, left at the age of about sev-
en*

*two cousins, left and center; au-
thor; and sister, right*

*Author's mother at home in vil-
lage of two thousand in Minnesota when he was fourteen*

To contact the author....

The author welcomes any and all comments and suggestions, and would very much enjoy chatting with you....

message@goldpogo.com

Author

Mt Mitchell North Carolina

Author a couple of years' back...

Refund policy

REFUND INFORMATION

Desire a refund? No problem: 100% refund, for any reason at all, and absolutely no questions asked, period. And no time limit on this offer. I recognize that sometimes, purchased items are discovered to simply not be a "good fit", or for any number of other reasons....

Loran Joly

If for any reason you desire a refund or desire to leave a comment,

please contact me at:

message@goldpogo.com

or

ReEnvision Press
Box #1036
1303 US 127 South
Suite 104
Frankfort, KY 40601